Sending Messages

Written by Jenny Feely
Photography by Michael Curtain

sundance™

Contents

Introduction

Every day, people talk and listen to each other. They tell each other what they are thinking. They send and receive messages.

Information is passed from one person to another. This is communication.

5

Talking to Each Other

People talk to communicate with each other. This is called verbal communication.

People also communicate with each other without using any words. They use their face and body. This is called body language.

When people talk to each other, they often use body language along with their words.

There are about 3,950 languages spoken in the world today. More people can speak the Chinese language than any other language.

Writing to Each Other

People write words to communicate. Written messages don't have to be memorized because people can read them again. A written message can be read a long time after it has been written.

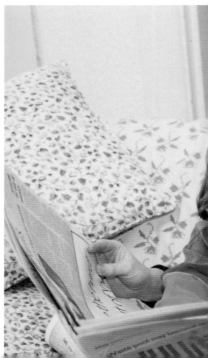

The oldest writing was invented over 5,000 years ago. People wrote on clay tablets and used pictures to represent words. We can use this writing to find out how people lived long ago.

Newspapers are a form of written communication that tell about events happening in the world. They use pictures, graphs, and maps, as well as words.

9

Telecommunications

People communicate with people in other places by using the telephone, radio, and television. These forms of communication need electricity to work.

Before telecommunications, people could only talk to each other if they were near each other.

A Scottish doctor, Alexander Graham Bell, invented the telephone in 1876. The first words he spoke on the telephone were to his assistant: "Mr. Watson, come here. I want you!"

Telecommunications: Radio

The first radio show was broadcast in the 1920s.

People use radio to communicate. At a radio station, sounds are turned into signals. These signals are transmitted and picked up when people turn on their radios.

Telecommunications: Television

Millions of people watch television. At a television station, pictures and sounds are turned into signals and transmitted. When a television is turned on, it picks up these signals.

Computers

People use computers to communicate. The Internet is a network of computers that links millions of computers around the world.

People use the Internet to send information to each other. People can use electronic mail (e-mail) to send messages to someone in the next room or on the other side of the world.

You can use e-mail to send the same message to lots of people at the same time.

E-mail messages only take a couple of seconds to send anywhere in the world. They can include pictures and sounds.

Satellites

Satellites receive and transmit telephone, radio, computer, and television signals around the world.

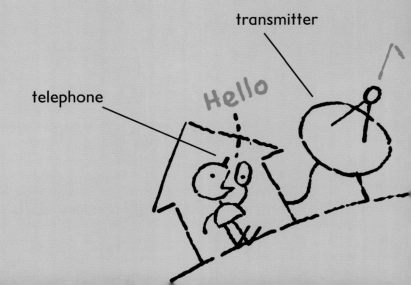

Satellites orbit the earth. Signals are beamed up to a satellite from a transmitter on earth. The satellite sends the signals back to a receiver on earth.

The first communications satellite was launched in 1960.

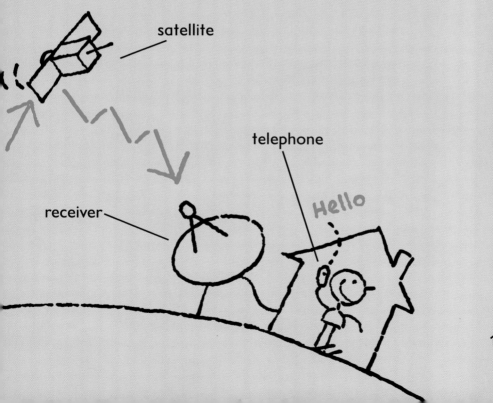

satellite

telephone

Hello

receiver

17

Imagining the Future

People are inventing newer and faster ways for communicating with each other every day. The "smart phone" can send and receive electronic postcards.

smart phone

electronic diary

18

Some mobile phones have video screens that allow a person to talk with a number of people at once.

What seems unimaginable today, might be everywhere tomorrow.

What next? Maybe a tiny telephone could be implanted in your head! Would that be a good idea?

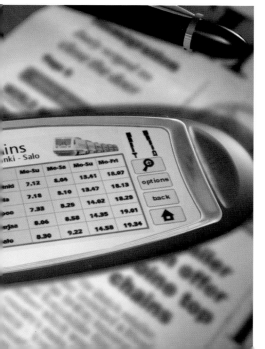

mobile video phone

Index